The Art of
Code Switching
in
(Black) America

By Michelle Weathersby, PCLC

The Art of Code-Switching in (Black) America, FIRST EDITION.

All credits appearing on the page or at the end of the book are considered an
extension of the copyright page.
Names: Weathersby, Michelle., author
Title: The Art of Code-Switching in (Black) America
Description: 1st edition. | Raleigh, NC: Michelle Weathersby Enterprises,
[2020]
Identifiers: ISBN-978-1-953175-00-7
Subjects: Business, Career Development, Leadership

The Internet addresses listed in the text were accurate at the time of
publication.

Contents

This book is dedicated to the greatest part of me – Jarrett, Kristin, Lauren, and Micah.

"Every great dream begins with a dreamer. Always remember, you have within you the strength, the patience, and the passion to reach for the stars to change the world"

~ HARRIET TUBMAN ~

Introduction

Why do we code-switch? It is so we can adequately communicate, so we fit in a place to get the desired result. Throughout this book, I will describe times that I have seen and been a part of to be a part of the crowd to achieve a desirable result. Believe it or not, we all have done it, but there are times that more cultures have to do it more than others that can cause pure frustration.

As our environment within our communities, the judicial system, religious practices, and corporate America show that injustice continues to happen that for change to occur, we have to find ourselves to be in a position to make the needed changes.

Let's venture together to see if we code-switch to accomplish a win, if it was automatic with no purpose or if we can really just be ourselves wherever we are.

What is Code Switching?

Have you found yourself speaking or acting differently around different groups of people? Do we do this to make them feel comfortable or for us to fit in the majority? Either way, it falls under the term of Code-Switching.

A code is a set of laws, regulations, and ideas or rules about how to behave.

The word switch is defined as an act of adopting one policy or way of life, or a change, especially a fundamental one.

The standard definition of Code-switching is when a person who speaks two or more languages uses these languages throughout a conversation to bring others into the conversation to bring comfort and belonging.

Code-switching is more than having a professional tone in a place of work. It is the ability to fit in and become a part of the group with less amount of issues or problems.

For African Americans and Black people in the United States, this may occur every day throughout to get through a day unscathed. I have always stated that God does not make mistakes, and I was made this way for a reason and purpose. Growing up in Detroit, Michigan, I grew up with the majority of the population being about 90% Black. Like many families around me, I did not think of color because most families had African, Native American, and European in the family tree . Hence, having relatives in different shapes and colors was never an issue until I got a little older and stepped away from the comfort of my family.

I was around 13 years old when I noticed my mother's voice changed during daily interaction with clients that were interested in the store she worked at that serviced customers for window treatments. It didn't matter who entered the store or called on the phone; she had "the voice."

This was not the first time I had heard "the voice," but it was at home and depended on who was on the other line of the phone, which was sometimes salespeople, and later, I found out they were bill collectors. She was able to turn it on and off so often that at times it became a regular occurrence.

I had to eventually ask her why she would change her voice at different times with people on the phone and in person. She told me, "People tend to respect Caucasian people in the business more than people of color." She learned this from her mother, who had moved from Tennessee with my grandfather and were more accepted due to their lighter skin complexion. I will briefly speak more on Color coding or Black color privilege in a later chapter.

The respect of the "White" voice was an incredible tool. The owner of the business my mother worked out was shocked that my mother was able to get some customers to pay on time when they usually did not pay. Sometimes when the customers came in, they would ask the women they were speaking to on the phone . They were astonished to find that it was my mother, while others were trying to figure out what race she was due to her lighter skin.

The business owner wanted my mother to continue being the receptionist, billing department, and operations for his business because it flourished so well. I remember listening to conversations she would have with the owner, and he did not want to pay her the skill set that she was utilizing, so she left.

Of course, I would not understand it all until I got older. My mother was underestimated as both a woman and a person of color. She knew how people had treated her differently compared to some of her darker-skinned siblings, so she was very aware of what was being present to her. He did ask her to come back, but he severely burned a bridge that could not be repaired.

I admired her courage and loyalty to herself as a person as she realized that she was given a gift that others perhaps would never discover in their lifetime.

So, a great way to think about what code-switching is listed below is what is needed to be successful in the implementation. As we go through the steps to be successful in an organization as a person of color, it is always important to know not to lose yourself. Your unique perspective is needed to help move a department or business to the next level of success.

C – Conceal

O – Opportunity

D – Deliver

E – Education

Workplace

The place where we work seems to be the most likely to be code-switching, especially if we are among the minority of the group, department, or organization.

This comes from a syndrome called "group think." It is a psychological phenomenon that occurs within a group of people in which the desire for harmony or conformity in the group results in an irrational or dysfunctional decision-making outcome.

In the current events, we can find many examples of this occurring both in our personal and professional lives. As we watch current events unfold due to race, some of us think about how we can change this, so perhaps our children or grandchildren do not have to experience the same heartbreak.

There are a few ways we can approach the problem. One way to approach the problem was displayed in a great movie to review and watch is "*Sorry To Bother You*." The story follows a young Black man who is a telemarketer and how just changing his voice to portray a White male allowed him to move up the corporate ladder and be privy to things that other employees were not allowed to access. Since it was a movie, some liberties were taken, but the message is clear on code-switching. This story also stated that if you are not careful that you can lose yourself pretending to be something you are not.

When my daughter started working in her field for the Air Force, she was told that she needed to scrub her voice, so when she is speaking on the radio that the listener should not be able to recognize her region within the United States. Everyone within the group, no matter the culture, had to sound very similar to Steve Colbert. He is a talk show host that has been able to master his voice to make it impossible to know where he lives or grew up. I don't understand the purpose of the exercise , but I know it was difficult for her because of her cultural background. She had begun for the strenuous process to create "the voice," so she would not be recognized.

Even though I did not encourage my children to change their voice for different situations, they were always able to detect if I spoke to a friend or someone professionally on the phone. I had to show the other part of the "professional persona."

One of the most beneficial times I had to use "the voice" was when I saw a posting position or a management position some years ago. It would require me to have the responsibility of 50 associates, a client's contract of $300M +, and in the process of being unfamiliar with the procedures the company was using. I was so excited to apply for this opportunity where I know I would make a positive contribution to the department and the company.

I did my research about the company and how they treated their diverse community. I was told from current employees in other locations that the company was not big on female or diversity in management.

This information was beneficial, but it did not deter me from applying and interviewing for the position.

During the interviewing process, I was able to disguise my race and obtain the job. Still, my manager, later on, was not happy to find out that I was Black even though we spoke several times during the interview process, and after I was hired. The face to face meeting that made everything clear.

Once I introduced myself as being the person he hired, he became physically upset and did not speak to me for the rest of the time he was there and even cut his trip short. Less than a week later, the executive vice president came down to see what I was doing. Even though I was preparing for some backlash, I was not ready to be warned by an executive manager that I was being watched very closely. I thought that saving the company $3 million in under 90 days would have shown my ability to strategize and lead, but it just seemed to add fuel to the fire that should have never been started. It was like I tricked them so I could have a better life.

In corporate America, you have to know when to use code-switching and when to turn it off, so you know who you are. There are times when some White people may have a pre-thought of what Black people are capable of and incapable of doing. Working with clients of different ages, genders, and cultural backgrounds, I have found that some individuals are hired on what they will produce. At the same time, Black people are employed on what they have already done, not future expectations, which limits their options for growth. If the latter is true, then it shows that there is no future really for a Black candidate since they are limited. The future is unwritten, so we do not know what a person can or can do, no matter their skin color.

Many of us have parents who wanted to insert Black heritage at the beginning of our lives by naming us something different from our White counterparts. This was acceptable within our communities, friends, and families. The roadblock occurred when we began to apply for college and work. Before the interviewer would even see us, they knew that we were Black. This, in itself, can take us out of the race before it even begins. "Despite laws against discrimination, affirmative action, a degree of employer enlightenment, and the desire by some businesses to enhance profits by hiring those most qualified regardless of race, African-Americans are twice as likely as whites to be unemployed, and they earn nearly 25 % less when they are employed."[1]

How can a person improve their work experience when they are not given the opportunity to do so?

What can be done about this? We need to be aware of this and take action to ensure we get hired in places that may only be stepping stones that are not within our original growth plan. I am sure that everyone may not agree with me on this point, but you have to get your foot in the door. Some ways that a couple of my clients and friends have

---

[1] https://www.nber.org/digest/sep03/w9873.html

gotten into the corporate positions were either by shortening their name to sound "more White" *(example: LaKresha changed to Reese)* or for them to use their initials *(example: LK)* instead of their name on their professional documents. Just like anything, some pros and cons are associated with these approaches. It is crucial to keep in mind what your goal is so you can be able to bring your whole self to work once you are in the organization so you can demonstrate your abilities.

We need to let others know we are not looking for a handout or charity when we have not done the work. We seek to have the equality that is provided for like our White counterparts, which in turn allows for us to care for our communities and families.

Now let us get some strategies that will allow us to move to the next level of success while being able for others to see who we really are.

Conceal

There are times that we may not want to be seen and just want to observe. It is key to be aware of your surroundings, so the proper response is given. To conceal is to keep something secret and prevent others from knowing who we are, come from, and sometimes our real thoughts.

Code-switching for many Americans of color has to be performed almost every day to bring peace and comfort to themselves and others who may not understand their race or culture.

Women in corporate American also do it as they climb up the ladder in the executive space.

According to the U.S. Department of Labor, there are 74.6 million women in the workforce, 47% of people working

[2]. The question that comes to my mind is that if so many people are in the minority who are working, then who are women and Black people trying to please or be like in corporate America, organizations, and communities.

In 2019 people of color made up 36.4% of the labor force. Breaking it down by race, Black/African American make up 12.3%, Asian makeup 6.5%, and 17.6% make up Hispanic or Latino.[3]

There are invisible guidelines in place that if a particular group of people responds like the people in power and prestige want them to, they will get noticed and climb the corporate ladder. With such a large number of people being different, how can anyone keep up?

Have you heard the term of someone being a chameleon before?

---

[2] https://www.bls.gov/cps/cpsaat03.htm
[3] https://www.bls.gov/cps/cpsaat18.pdf

The definition of a chameleon is a lizard (the *lizard that changes its colors regularly is an example of a chameleon)* that can change colors to match its surroundings or a person who varies their personality depending on who they are with or the type of personality they are around.

There are many times people of color and women have to hide who they are and have to change their "stripes" dialects, enunciating words, and sometimes when they find something funny or when to respond to comments that are being made about others.

When working for this fortune 500 company, there were many stipulations on Black people compared to other White people. It was very evident when the new interns would come into the corporation annually. Usually, out of a cohort of 50 students that there would be one Black male, two Asian or Latino females, and the rest were

White. This subject was brought to senior and executive management's attention, from several other Black co-workers, and a White colleague. The reasoning we received was that there were not any good candidates in the job market or college institutions.

As I was able to research the issue a bit further, it was discovered that a physiological test was being given to all the interns and geared more favorable to White students. Once I spoke with the director, who was bringing in the students and the human resource department that the test was removed from the hiring process. This allowed an increase of minority candidates to increase by 3%.

During this change process, I was able to sit with several hiring managers bringing in candidates from the surrounding colleges. We had to rate the students on how they would react and behave to different project management that was given to the students. I remember one instance where a young White female and young Black male both displayed the same characteristics of taking charge to get the tasks completed according to the directions we gave them.

After completing the tasks, it was stated that the young lady was a go-getter, and the young man was aggressive and a bully to his other teammates. Since I was able to witness both candidates in action, I had to call a spade a spade. I pointed out the managers' assessment of both of the candidate's performance and how they demonstrated racial bias, perhaps without not even recognizing it.

This young man was able to get hired because I was in the room to speak up for him. We may have to stay concealed until the situation requires an unpopular response.

If you are reading this, you may be thinking that perhaps the young lady had a better resume, extra-curricular activities, or community service. This was not an issue because, for any candidate to be invited for a call back during this time for testing, they had to have reached stated guidelines across the board.

I know how important it is to access groups that make decisions that may be affecting your well-being along with others, and then you have to decide what is the best response for the situation.

How often are you finding yourself Code-Switching a month, a week, a day? List your events below.

_____

_____

_____

_____

_____

_____

_____

_____

_____

_____

_____

_____

_____

_____

_____

_____

_____

_____

_____

Opportunity

Many opportunities come our way through circumstances that make it possible to do something as an individual or a team. This is the time to display our gifts and skillsets.

Have you found yourself presented a chance to make a difference in an area that you would not have been a part of unless someone brought you in? We are given these

opportunities so we can help others reach their goals .

Playing by the rules within a particular community can be both exhausting and rewarding. You have to be able to conform, so others know that you have the ability to take the organization to where it needs to go.

As a person who has grown up in the heart of an inner-city, went to school , and was able to obtain a position in an executive management role, it has allowed me to see different stages of opportunities and appreciate what is offered.

It is essential to understand that we have to answer to someone with the rules or guidelines in different areas of our lives. Everything may not line up in favorable circumstances, for we believe the requirement of success, but we need to grasp those changes to put ourselves to the forefront. Having the confidence and courage to move into spaces that only a few of us may have the opportunity to be in is important for other Black team members who may not have the change will get one now because we can move forward.

There are times when it is apparent that we are the "one diverse" team member and know the group states that now they have achieved diversity. Once you recognize this "gift" - yes, I called it a gift , learn everything you can about what the position entails so you can help others who are looking to get advice from you on how to get where you are. You do not want them to be ambushed with unpreparedness. Despite popular belief, there are many times that we do become our brother's (sister's) keeper.

Our season of being comfortable in just what we know has passed. The meaning of being comfortable is being at ease, relaxed, and content. There is nothing wrong with being comfortable because it provides safety and peace - but does it? After I got my Bachelor's degree, I soon discovered that I needed to obtain my Master's degree and other certifications ⬚ . So now, I must get

uncomfortable with putting funds aside to pay for courses,

carve out time to study, and still have time for family.

It is time for us to expand and grow, so…...

LET'S GET UNCOMFORTABLE!!!

Have you missed opportunities that could have taken you to the next level? What do you plan to do differently next time?

_____

_____

_____

_____

_____

_____

_____

_____

_____

_____

_____

_____

_____

_____

Deliver

It may time for you to produce what you stated that would be completed within a specific time agreed upon. Because you are a person of color, this delivery may be more harshly judged compared to your non-black counterparts. A few things, listed below that need to be remembered is to review the expectations from the reviewer to ensure that when you are presenting that you are meeting their expectation and then go beyond that whenever possible.

- Understand the vision of a project/assignment.

- Know who the stakeholders are and aware of the business values.

- You may have to research the group you are working with to know how to respond appropriately during meetings and interactions.

Keeping this in mind is essential, so you do not have to do double work due to a lack of communication.

Unfortunately, you may be getting compared to other people of color and just not on your merits of what you have provided in the past. As stated in the workplace chapter, the manager may be taking a "chance" on you because of color.

This is something that we should not have to think about, but it should not be forgotten.

Working in corporate America, I would see this often happen to people who were not a particular age group, gender, culture, or race. A great example was for this occurring was is when there were two women who had plans set up in place before getting hired for this company I had worked in the past. The first woman was Black and over 40, and she had made plans to see an ailing sister. The other woman was White and 27 with plans to get married. I assured both ladies as their direct manager and executive management that their vacations would be honored when it was time for their time off with agreement from human resources (HR) and executive management.

Right before each person's vacation, there were big deadlines that developed because of changes in policies and procedures. Due to the airplane, hotel, and destination plan, neither could cancel without it cost them extra money financially and of course, psychology this would not be great team morale if they missed their commitments.

As their manager, I had to go to HR to get an exception for each person's vacation to go through because executive management instructed me that any time off for employees had to be suspended to ensure the deadline was reached. The White young lady was able to go with no issues while the Black lady had a write up against her for not being able to work during an essential business need. Other team members were willing to work to cover the needed deadlines for their teammates. This action had set a negative standard for the team's morale, and after a while, a few of the teammates told me that they did not feel safe with the company anymore, so they quit.

In this last scenario, both ladies took the needed steps in the beginning to ensure compliance for their department and company, but more was required of the Black lady.

As a rule of thumb, leaders want all of their followers to do an excellent job for the department and company projects. And sometimes the consequences of when we don't can be significant.

I was employed at a corporation where I experienced this firsthand. I would first state that I was at fault, along with several others, for a mistake that occurred on a large client's account. There were missed items from every department, and everyone was trying to cover themselves on who was most at fault. I picked the short straw. Even though I informed the group about the issues on a few different occasions, I told them later that I did not aggressively pursue the matter to the right people, which is why the company had to let me go. Looking at all of the major players of this project, I was the only Black leader overall. It didn't matter if my percentage of misdirection was smaller compared to the others-someone had to lose their job. The lesson learned here was everyone makes mistakes learn from the mistakes and document everything!

I was upset with the decision but knew the environment I

had been working in for a while. I dropped the ball

on being diligent and got tired. I knew on previous

occasions, my White male manager had been reported to

human resources already for mismanagement of

employees and procedures from several employees of all

races, including myself, and nothing had been done about

it. I told myself that I just didn't care anymore – of course

this is the wrong attitude to display, and I paid a heavy

penalty for it.

Within a year, over half of the team quit after I was gone,

and the manager was reassigned to a new position with a

raise. Such is life.

Remember, delivery can look very different from others

depending on what their bias is about that person, and

sometimes that race of people.

Being ready and knowing who you are working for will help to allow for you to strategize to win.

Are you delivering what you have promised? What is stopping you from over-delivering?

_____

_____

_____

_____

_____

_____

_____

_____

_____

_____

_____

_____

_____

_____

_____

Education

Gaining knowledge is one of the greatest tools a person can earn to move forward in any situation. Establishing a formal education is one way for a lot of Black people to move forward in corporate America. In job postings, we have seen what is required within the education section of needed skills from a candidate to obtain this kind of job. Many of us attended colleges and training to gain information about a particular field or subject.

Education can come in many ways. Formal and informal. Some positions state that a degree is needed or certification, but what it does not state is some of this education may be bypassed by having a mentor, sponsor, and advisor to help you connect with the overall decision-maker.

There are times that we have seen and even experienced White team members being promoted to positions that they are not experienced in or even hold any kind of degree in that industry. So, I get the question of "why should I even get a degree if I am not going to get the job?".

First, once you receive that piece of paper, then it can be taken away from anyone, and you know that you were able to accomplish this goal in your life, allowing others to see your success.

Second, even though it may not open a door that you may want right now, it has opened doors that may not have otherwise been opened.

Going through training and having a degree signals to others that you are coachable and have the will to do better and want better.

According to US News Today, "among minorities, all ethnic groups' career earnings were less than that of Caucasians, save for Asians with Master's, doctoral, and professional degrees, who outpaced white workers with degrees of the same level. Latinos and African-Americans with Master's degrees earn nearly the same in their lifetimes—roughly $2.50 million—as white workers who have Bachelor's degrees."[4]

There are quite a few employers who are willing to reimburse their employees to go gain an educational degree or even a certification.

Even though there are rules to knowing the CODE, it is equally important to know who you are so you will not lose yourself into something someone else wants you to

---

[4] https://www.usnews.com/education/best-colleges/articles/2011/08/05/how-higher-education-affects-lifetime-salary

be. Being the best version of yourself only occurs with continued growth.

LET'S GET EDUCATED - Don't leave money on the table!

Are you hesitating about going back to school or taking a training course? Write down all the advantages of obtaining this from a better job to a sense of accomplishment.

_____

_____

_____

_____

_____

_____

_____

_____

_____

_____

_____

_____

_____

_____

_____

_____

_____

What is Emotional Intelligence (EQ)?

Every person has a degree of Emotional Intelligence (EQ), just like Intelligence Quotient (IQ). With practice and studying, people can increase their scores in both areas, but some people have been blessed with higher intelligence based on their gifts and talents. EQ is when a person has the capacity to be aware of, control, express one's emotions, and handle interpersonal relationships judiciously and empathetically.

This is a person, usually, the vast majority of people like. They can connect at almost any level of people or organizations once they listen to the conversation and interact with them. The higher the EQ, the more likely and easier it is to adapt to the current environment without losing who it is.

According to Daniel Goleman, author of Emotional Intelligence 2.0, it is vital to display certain key elements to begin a successful emotional intelligence. Listed below are ways that we can start to learn about others and also help us to respond to situations in both our personal and business lives.

- **Self-awareness** is being conscious and knowledgable of one's character, feelings, motives, and desires and knowing your dislikes and likes.

  When a person knows themselves, then they can help others express how they feel. This is great when you know that you can be open without being penalized when speaking the truth.

- **Self-regulation** entails acting under your long-term goals and deepest values. For example, you find it challenging to eat healthy consistently even though you may feel better each time that you do, so you have to discipline yourself.

We keep networking or interacting with different organizations until a goal is met, no matter how mundane it may seem. Any connections are a great connection. It can be nurtured for long-term or short-term relationships. There are times at work that it seems our conversations go unnoticed by co-workers, but they are watching and taking notes.

- **Empathy** is the ability to understand and share the feelings of another.

Understanding different situations and how people can react to them helps you to respond correctly to a person. Displaying a sensitivity towards a family matter or work situation will allow you to create a stronger relationship with people.

We feel comfortable when we have people around us who have similar ideas and concepts and seem to understand us as a person.

- **Social skills** are talents we use every day to interact and communicate with others, including verbal and non-verbal communication, such as speech, gesture, facial expression, and body language. The process of learning these skills is called socialization, and a lack of such skills can cause social awkwardness.

Knowing what your win helps with what kind of persona you will be bringing to the table. The proper response to a question or situation will allow others to see what are your leadership skills. Having personal and professional conversations with people gives you an insight into what is happening in their community.

Even though everyone does not treat us right, if we have an idea of what is happening in their lives, then we can have a more constructive and positive response to that person or a situation with that person in it.

What are your EQ strengths and weaknesses?

_____

_____

_____

_____

_____

_____

_____

_____

_____

_____

_____

_____

_____

_____

_____

_____

Cracking The Code

When will people of color be allowed to be themselves in all environments? What is the "key" to the lock to release the code? There are times that I still find that I have to code-switch two to three times a day. Yes, it becomes exhausting.

I grew up in Michigan on the westside of Detroit, which was not easy by any means. My parents were heavy in the traditional church guidelines, so we spoke differently and dressed differently from many of our friends and classmates. There were two competing gangs in my neighborhood that always tried to recruit my siblings and me weekly.

You see, my parents had eight children – 4 girls and 4 boys, and we were considered to be the pick of the litter because if one sibling decided to join the gang, then the other soon would follow. This could have been successful, but my dad was a preacher, so it was more than his eyes that were watching over us.

Since it was known that we were "church kids," we got picked on constantly from kids in the neighborhood and school. So, to fit in, we would say and do things to help to ease the teasing and bullying. We began speaking as if we were a part of the streets to let others know we knew what they were talking about, and we were the same as them.

Of course, this was not always effective because we were extremely limited in our television watching and radio listening, so we were caught "pretending" to know.

There were times when we were physically harmed, or my parent's property was damaged. I had made promises to myself that my children would not have to live in an environment that would harm their bodies or creativity.

As my dad got promoted, my parents were able to move us out outside of Detroit. So now we want to be surrounded by 98% Black people to 99.5% Caucasian. Honestly, I was not sure which environment was scarier to live in. My new surroundings consisted of a lot of confederate flag believers.

As we began to attend school in this area, we found that we were accepted because we spoke the same dialect language as the students in the area. It seemed to amaze them that we looked different but understood what they were talking about most of the time.

As I was able to get comfortable and formulate friendships, I was able to ask why it was fascinating to have friends who were Black. It was explained that he behaved nothing like the people who they saw on television but not quite like people in the area.

Needless to say, we had a few run-ins with people who thought we didn't belong there, but they didn't realize that the idle threats were less intimidating than living in Detroit.

I thought a lot of turmoil was over until my husband and I moved to North Carolina. We both became acutely aware of how officials felt about people of color, especially the males.

With having four children, a mixture of sons and daughters, I became blatantly aware of the bias that they teachers were treating my sons, and I had to be their advocates to stop the foolishness on so many levels.

After a few phone calls and face-to-face conferences, school seemed to run smoother for my son until he started driving.

My husband and I took him to drivers' education for him to learn the North Carolina rules of the road while at the same time teaching him the "black man" rules of the road.

If a law enforcement officer is prompting you to pull over at any time, one of the vital first steps is to not reach for your wallet, registration, or anything else other than the steering wheel. This allows the officer to view that you are willing to comply with the next steps, usually asking for your driver's license and registration. Some of you may be thinking – why cannot they get these things while waiting for the officer to come to the window. In American history, this has shown to be vital for the driver on several occasions.

As my son continues living his life as a college student under the age of 25 that he has had individual and group interaction with the police at least five times that he has told me about. Some of us over 40 have not even been pulled over more than three times. My son has a title called "driving while Black" is unfortunately what he has to be careful every time he has to go work, school, vacation, dining out and even church.

Any deviation from the "black man" rules of the road could end up in immediate and permanent harm. This is when code-switching and behavior is truly a life and death lesson that will have to follow my sons for the rest of their lives as current history continues to demonstrate the cruelty from others.

As you read about some of my story above, did you have to go through something similar? How were you able to survive?

_____

_____

_____

_____

_____

_____

_____

_____

_____

_____

_____

_____

_____

_____

_____

What lessons could you take from the streets to survive and achieve the next level of your life?

_____

_____

_____

_____

_____

_____

_____

_____

_____

_____

_____

_____

_____

_____

_____

_____

Let's Grow Together

If you did not learn anything from growing up as a child, then the chances are that you may have to repeat the same lesson as an adult, and we know that when we are doing a retest that the questions on the test have changed and sometimes have become more difficult.

So, the question to ask is if we were allowed to bring our "whole self" to different environments, would we be accepted? I would have said that it would be yes for some and no for others. It is a gamble that some are willing to take, no matter the cost. We have to evaluate our risk tolerance and how much we are willing to put on the line so others can succeed.

Part of learning how to use the power of sound. In my book The Art of (Black) Executive Presence, we explore the importance of making yourself known and established in the management space utilizing:

- **Pitch** - is the quality of a sound governed by the rate of vibrations producing its quality and strength.

- **Pace** - the speed or rate at which how fast you are speaking and how it can display a certain amount of confidence.

- **Tone** - is the general character or attitude and the feel of an environment attitude, and is it reflected in a person's behavior.

- **Volume** – are you bringing the correct degree of loudness that shows confidence.

- **Materials** – supplying your audience the needed facts through quality means.

Hopefully, you have been making notes throughout this book. We need to dig deep and find why we are code-switching or understand why others feel that they need to code-switch.

In the end, if we want to continue to grow and move forward, we will need to "Adapt or Die."

Bias Questions You Maybe Asking Yourself – write down the first thought that comes to your mind then review it to see if it is viable and if it is not, then write down why you believe you feel this way. These answers can be a part of the beginning of positive change.

Can people of color bring value to the table? Can other cultures bring value to the table?

_____

_____

_____

_____

_____

_____

_____

_____

_____

_____

_____

_____

Why and am I afraid to diversify my professional and personal circles/communities?

_____

_____

_____

_____

_____

_____

_____

_____

_____

_____

_____

_____

_____

_____

_____

_____

Why do I get upset if someone of a different age (younger/older), gender or race becomes my superior?

_____

_____

_____

_____

_____

_____

_____

_____

_____

_____

_____

_____

_____

_____

_____

_____

_____

Do I really want everyone (who I work with, interact with) to be just like me?

_____

_____

_____

_____

_____

_____

_____

_____

_____

_____

_____

_____

_____

_____

_____

_____

"The goal in any communication, especially business, is to control how other people perceive you when you speak."

Remember, you only have a few seconds for people to decide if they believe you and want to listen to what you are going to say next.[5]

---

5 https://www.forbes.com/sites/raquelbaldelomar/2017/04/19/five-strategies-to-help-you-sound-like-the-leader-you-want-to-be/#825f6d830ffb

CONTACT INFORMATION

LinkedIn: https://www.linkedin.com/in/michelle-weathersby-leadership-executive-career-coaching-consulting/

Facebook: https://www.facebook.com/LENSConsultingFirm/

Twitter: @lenscareer

Instagram: lens.career

Website: michelleweathersby.com

Email: michelle.weathersby@outlook.com

Books & Resources

The Art of Code-Switching in (Black) America Journal

The Art of (Black) Executive Presence Journal

The Art of Parent/Child Leadership Conversations Journal

The Art of (Black) Executive Presence

The Art of …. Parent/Child Leadership Conversation Series

About Michelle Weathersby

Michelle Weathersby is certified and degreed as an Executive Leadership Career Life Coach, Quality Improvement Associate/Process Master, Women Leadership Studies, Corporate Diversity & Inclusion Trainer, and Human Resource Management.

Through her education and experience, she works with clients by positioning them to receive the career strategies, leadership skills, and financial backing desired by advising them on professional profiles and platforms through LinkedIn™ Profiles, Press Releases, Coaching, Media Kits & Resumes along with other career development services. Michelle enjoys helping individuals and organizations to leverage their skills and talents to achieve their desired goals by collaborating with diverse teams of professionals to accomplish new levels of success in a variety of highly competitive industries.

Made in USA - Kendallville, IN
1221571_9781953175007